D1520465

Joy in *Jumping*

Joy in *Jumping*

A Mother's Journey *through* Grief

VIRGINIA PATTON

Purpose House Publishing

Published by PurposeHouse Publishing, Columbia, Maryland (www.purposehousepublishing.com). Cover Design by PurposeHouse Publishing.

Printed in the USA.

ISBN: 9798391043300

For Jeffrey

My beautiful son, Jeffrey William Patton (March 19, 1993 - March 23, 2022),

I wrote this book for you, anyone who has lost someone they love, and, most importantly, my wonderful Lord and Savior, Jesus Christ. He has been my hope, comfort, and healing throughout this past year. And for your dad and siblings who have shared the journey of grief with me. Their love and support have been unwavering.

Jeffrey, we'll love you forever.

"Holding grief simultaneously with God's goodness feels impossible. But in Joy in Jumping, Virginia Patton finds a way to honestly hold the two in tandem. Through Virginia's journey, the reader discovers a path between despair and loss. By consistently acknowledging God amidst her grief, Virginia illuminates a path of hope."

— Benjamin Long M.D.

Contents

Foreword

Each one of us has suffered loss along the way but not all of us has suffered well. Beloved, I urge you to grab hold of the chapters of this treasured heartfelt account of a mother who courageously speaks, "My God Is Sovereign!" Virginia's words pour forth an invitation to face the ugliest of truths while choosing to see the mighty hand of God through it all. Ponder the questions that are beautifully appointed throughout as you too encounter God as you grieve. Corrie Ten Boom once said, "There is no pit that God's love isn't deeper still."

Virginia has taken her great loss and has released hope, faith, and love throughout the pages of her book. In all honesty, she being the catalyst has released a legacy as her son Jeffrey's life still speaks as the reader reads, prayers, and ponders the honest thoughts, feelings, and emotions of losing someone so precious while all the while birthing new life, fresh hope, greater grace, and seeing the goodness of God . . . always.

Sarah Gennusa, author of Pearls from the Heart, wife to Bryan Gennusa, mother of four biological children and one adopted child, American missionary to Alaska, India and nations beyond.

Acknowledgements

Jess, Josh, Josiah, Justin, Jacob, Jeremy, Heather, and Koren, I love you, and I am so thankful for you. We each carry our grief differently, but I have witnessed your grace and faith as you have endured losing Jeffrey. I know he has left his mark on each of your lives, and through you, he lives on. I want you to know I am praying for you always and am immensely proud of you.

James, I love you so very much. Jeffrey was beyond blessed to have you as a father. You were always there, at every game; no matter how tired you were, you always took time to throw the football around with the boys. You are an incredible man of God, and I have seen your strong faith through this unbearable loss. You have been my strength as I know you pray for me. This has gotten me through many hard days. You are the best person I know, and I am so blessed to walk through this life with you. Thank you for all you do for me and, most of all, for being my rock.

I want to also thank my best friend, Laura, who has been there for me this past year. You have always had kind, encouraging words and a soft shoulder for me to cry on. So many times, you knew how I was feeling without a word. Thank you for the countless hugs, love, and tears you graciously shared with me. I love you.

I would be amiss if I didn't include my wonderful editor and new friend, Bonnie McNeal. Thank you for your encouragement, wisdom, and guidance. Your kind words have confirmed to my soul that God will use this book to help hurting people.

Thank you, Jesus, for your love. Thank you for your Word. Thank you for rescuing me when I was drowning under the waters of grief. Thank you for pulling me to safety, wrapping your arms around me, and giving me strength.

Most of all, I thank you, Lord, for Jeffrey. Thank you for blessing our family by giving us such a beautiful son, brother, and friend. It was an honor and joy to be his mother; I am eternally grateful for this.

I pray, Lord, you use these words to help a mother, father, sister, brother, or friend who must go through grief. I pray this will encourage them to look up to you, for that is where our help comes from. Speak to them through your Word as you did with me as they lay their grief at your feet.

Thank you, Lord, for all you are, our eternally loving Father whose love lifts us out of the darkness and into your arms of comfort and hope.

1

HE WAS AS SURPRISED AS WE WERE

Wednesday, March 23, 2022, was a normal day. I went to work, came home, ate dinner, took a bath, and did all the normal things. My sweet husband was at church leading our weekly Bible study, so I was home alone that evening. I remember sitting in my chair when my phone rang. I looked at the caller ID and saw it was Josh, my oldest son. I am always excited to talk to him, so I answered it on the first or second ring. The first thing he did was ask me if I was alone. He asked where his dad was. I thought that was strange, and something about him sounded off. He was choked up and was having difficulty speaking. I immediately sensed there was a problem, and my mind went to a hundred different scenarios. I started rapidly firing questions at him . . . what's wrong? Are the kids ok? Are you sick? Did something happen? His response to my questions was something I had never dreamed of in my wildest dreams I would ever hear. He gently proceeded to tell me something had happened to Jeffrey. My first thought was he was involved in a car accident. The next words that I heard are words to this day I am not sure I heard right. He choked out, "Mom, he's gone." I said, "What do you mean, he's gone, gone where?" He then said, "Mom, Jeffrey passed." My brain couldn't register those words, and I know my heart didn't understand.

I realize now that was the hardest phone call Josh ever had to make, and I still hurt for him. I wish I could have protected him from such heartache. I wish I could have protected us all.

The rest of that evening was a blur. My other children who lived nearby came over immediately to be with me as we all gathered in shock. I distantly remember hearing their voices, but it sounded like they were in an echo chamber. They quickly planned to take me to my daughter's house so we could wait for their dad to come home from Bible study. Nothing could have prepared me for this moment.

I vaguely remember telling my husband what had happened, but I'll never forget the look of shock on his face. It was the worst day of my life, the worst day of all our lives.

Questions formed in my heart and mind instantly. I needed to know exactly what had happened. Jeffrey had just celebrated his 29th birthday on March 19th. This just couldn't be true. He was healthy, strong, and young. He was a runner, often running very long distances just for the love of it. He was in the best shape of his life. How did this happen? I saw the same questions on the faces of his dad, brothers, and sister . . . how?

It would be a very long time before we got an answer to that question. The next day we spoke with the police officer on the scene and got a clearer picture of what happened. He told us a co-worker found Jeffrey after going to his apartment. She called 911, and the paramedics arrived, but it was too late. Jeffrey had already been gone for too long. He told us they found him face down on the floor, clutching a blanket around his heart. It appeared that Jeffrey had a massive heart attack. He said there were no signs of outward trauma, and it didn't appear that he had intentionally hurt himself. The next thing he said was burned in my mind. He said, "Ma'am, your son was just as surprised as you are." That was it. No reason. Just an awful surprise. How do I go on? How do we go on?

2

IT'S NOT RIGHT

In the weeks that followed, I found myself repeating the same thought to myself: "It's not right." It's not right that a young, healthy, sweet young man just dropped dead alone in his apartment. It's not right that his two older brothers had to go clean out his belongings and had to bear the unbearable pain of walking into the scene of their brother's last breath. It's not right that I didn't get to tell him I love him one more time. It's not right that he will never fall in love, get married, have children, and grow old. It's not right that the world gets to go on while my family and I are standing still in this nightmare. I want to scream out, "It's not right, it's not right. *It's not right!*"

 In the early weeks and months after his death, these thoughts haunted my waking moments. There will always be thoughts of "it's not right" tumbling around in my heart, probably for the rest of my earthly life. Even as I write this, I think it's not right that I have to write this book. But it's something I must do, something I'm compelled to do. Maybe my experience will help someone else, or maybe the process of getting these thoughts down on paper will somehow be therapeutic for me. But I know the most important reason I'm filling these pages with my pain, trauma, and grief is because of Jeffrey. He wanted to help people. This is a way for him to do that.

I've been trying to shift my mindset lately, focusing on the blessings God has given me, such as my husband and my other beautiful children and grandchildren. I identify with King David when he wrote these comforting words. "Even though I walk through the valley of the shadow of death, I will fear no evil, for you are with me: your rod and your staff, they comfort me" (Psalm 23:1-4 ESV).

Believe me, death is a valley. Anyone who has lost someone they love understands the shadow death casts. But I've come to realize that even though I must walk through this valley and experience the shadow my son's death has created, I can fear no evil. I know God's word and love surround and comfort me every minute of every day. God's light and love penetrate the darkness and give me confidence that His goodness and mercy follow me all the days of my life.

I believe God is good, no matter what happens in our lives. God's character is goodness and love. He cannot change. God is good to me, my family, and Jeffrey. Even though there are times I can't understand or see God's goodness in this, God's character doesn't change. He understands when I can't. He comforts me when I'm inconsolable. He loves me in and through all things. I can rest in His goodness and, like David, declare that God is with me in this valley.

— Reflection —

What are your "it's not right" feelings? God longs
to heal these for you. How does God's Word
comfort you during these times?

_____

_____

_____

_____

_____

_____

_____

3

THE HARDEST TIME OF DAY

The other night I was thinking about how bedtime is one of the hardest times of my day. It's when I'm still that my thoughts always go to Jeffrey. If I'm honest, it seems every moment of every day is hard, but the evenings are definitely the hardest. It's at night that my sorrow seems to take on physical attributes as I reach out in the dark to the One who can give me peace. It's a peace that passes all understanding because I certainly don't understand this. I'm learning I can experience God's peace in my heart even though my brain is clouded with unanswered questions. In the dark, I try to pray, but I cannot find the words. It's at those times I feel God's peace settle on me, and again I am reminded that He knows my heart. He hears the groanings of my spirit, and He's always there.

One of the most gracious experiences I have had in all of this is that just when I need it most, God sends me a dream of my precious Jeffrey. He is always smiling, always happy, and always silly. I can hug him, touch him, smell him. He always tells me he is fine, he is happy, and that I have nothing to be sad about. It's the kind of dream I don't want to wake up from.

It's dreams like this that remind me death is not permanent.

> *I tell you the solemn truth, the*
> *one who hears my message and*
> *believes the one who sent me*
> *has eternal life and will not be*
> *condemned, but has crossed*
> *over from death to life.*
> *(John 5:24 NET)*

12

*Because, if you confess with
your mouth that Jesus is Lord
and believe in your heart that
God raised him from the dead,
you will be saved.
(Romans 10:9 NET)*

Jeffrey believed; Jeffrey confessed. He told his father and me that on a beautiful Saturday afternoon. He came out of his room and walked up to us, and told us that he had finally prayed. He had grown tired of trying to cope with life's struggles on his own, and he understood his own sins had led to many problems in his young life. He realized that he needed God's forgiveness. He needed to repent. I knew that no matter what Jeffrey experienced from that moment on, he was not alone. He had his faith, and with that, he could move forward. It wasn't long after that day my sweet son died, and it gives me such comfort to know I will see him again. He didn't really get a chance to grow in his faith, but like the thief on the cross, Jeffrey heard the words, "Today you will be with Me in Paradise."

◆——— Reflection ———▶

My hardest time of day is ...

_____

_____

_____

_____

_____

_____

_____

4

GOD DECIDES

Since Jeffrey's death, there have been many times I think about what God might do next. I believe God is Sovereign. I believe He has total control of all things past, present, and future. Nothing happens outside of His knowledge. In other words, God decides. God knew about Jeffrey's birth and death before I did. I understand that nothing can end our lives before God ordains it. He knew about every moment in Jeffrey's life where he felt fear, pain, or struggle. He knew how Jeffrey's death would impact my family and me. How it would change

17

us, change how we think on a daily basis. Every day, thoughts of Jeffrey come to my mind constantly.

I often think of Job from the Bible. As I read through this biblical account, I saw a transformation. Job's understanding of God changed, and, as a result, my understanding changed as well. It was hard for me to look through my grief and see the Sovereignty of God. It took me a while as I contemplated the loss of my beloved son.

I mentioned earlier that I was afraid of what God might do next. It was my thought that God took Jeffrey so quickly, so easily; what else might He do? One moment my life was good and free of troubles, and the next moment I was devastated. I was crushed. It was God's right to take Jeffrey. I fully believe this. I just didn't want him to. I found myself begging God not to take my other children. I think through these heartfelt thoughts, I developed a healthy fear of God.

Proverbs 9:10 states, "The fear of the Lord is the beginning of wisdom," but I didn't want this kind of wisdom. It took me a minute to accept this. I think *believing* in the Sovereignty of God and accepting the Sovereignty of God are quite different. It's easy to say things like "God has a plan" or "All things work together for good to those who love God and are called according to His purposes," but to accept these truths takes time and personal surrender.

Personal surrender is something we humans are not prone to do. It's not a problem when everything is going our way, and we are getting everything we want. But it's different when something crashes into our reality, and we are drowning under its weight. At least, that was my experience. But God is good, God is patient, God is loving. He was there in my valley teaching me and giving me grace to face each tomorrow. He helped me understand His Sovereignty. Like Job, I can say to God, "I know that you can do all things; no purpose of yours can be thwarted"

19

(Job 42:1-2). So with Job, I say, "The Lord gives, and the Lord takes away, May the name of the Lord be blessed!" (Job 1:21).

◆———— Reflection ————◆

What must I surrender in my grief process?

_____

_____

_____

_____

_____

_____

_____

_____

5

JOY IN THE JUMPING

When my children were small, it was natural for them to trust me. Any parent knows this as they stand in the deep end of the pool and beckon their child to jump into their arms. Parents are sure to catch them as they plunge into the deep dark water. It's up to the child to believe this, to keep their eyes on the parent, and simply trust and jump. In the jumping, they learn that someone who loves them is right there waiting, watching, encouraging them to let go of fear.

I have strong memories of Jeffrey standing at a pool's edge, gathering up his courage to jump into my arms. It only took one time for him to realize he was safe, which led him to jump over and over and over again! Soon he was jumping in by himself, knowing I always had my eye on him. He felt safe, confident, and protected by this truth. I smile now as I remember his Tarzan yell as he ran and jumped in the pool. He would scream, "Mom, watch!" then take off running and plunge himself into the pool. As his head ascended out of the water, his eyes were always on me to make sure I had seen his feat of daring. He had no thought of his own safety because he rested his trust in me. He would come up out of the water laughing and giddy with joy in the jumping.

This leads me to ask myself, *Do I trust my Heavenly Father as much?* Do I stand in the truth that even if I jump into deep dark waters, He will be there watching, protecting, and pulling me to safety? That is exactly how grief feels most of the time—like deep, dark waters pulling me under. I always thought I trusted God, but when He took Jeffrey home, my world was rocked. I had to face my faith head-on. What did I believe? What did I stand on? Was it a house of sand, or was it a house built on solid rock?

The answer came as more of a resolve in my soul than a response to questions. My faith is not built on anything less than Jesus Christ, my Savior, who died for me. I know He cares for me no matter what comes into my life because He is Sovereign because He loves me unconditionally.

> *The rain fell, the flood came,*
> *and the winds beat against that*
> *house, but it did not collapse*
> *because its foundation had been*
> *laid on rock.*
> *(Matthew 7:25)*

He has His eyes on me wherever I go now and forever. That is why when I am plunged into the dark waters of grief, I will reach out for His loving arms. He pulls me to safety, keeps my head above the water, and holds me up when I feel I am going under. I can trust in Him. I am learning to be like Jeffrey and to have joy in the jumping.

—————•————— Reflection —————•—————

How has God pulled me out of the waters of my grief?

_____

_____

_____

_____

_____

_____

_____

_____

6

MANIFESTO

I have done lots of soul-searching throughout my grief journey. I have also learned a lot about myself, my faith, and others. I felt it was important to include in this book my own realizations as a kind of personal statement of beliefs. It's good to write these kinds of things down, a declaration of faith and resolve. I have included this for you, Reader, in the hopes that it will encourage you to take time and consider your own beliefs. Write them down, and post them on your mirror or wall in your home. I know there will be many times grief will rear its ugly head, and Satan will use that to tear you down. He wants you to feel hopeless and give up. But you can't give in to his lies. Truth is Truth, and God's Truth will guide you through this. I have included my statement or manifesto of sorts in hopes it will bless you and encourage you to do the same.

I believe...

I believe God is good, not some of the time but all the time. I believe God is good to me, to my husband, and to my children, no matter what circumstances we may experience. I believe God is Sovereign. Nothing happens to me outside of His knowledge and control; therefore, I can trust in Him completely.

I will thank God for giving me Jeffrey, for allowing me to be his mom, and for teaching me important lessons through his life. I will praise God in the taking as much as I did in the giving. I will never charge God with wrong for taking my son, but rather I will praise Him for Jeffrey's life.

30

I will accept this pain as I have accepted so many joys.

I will keep my eyes on the Cross, making the things of this world grow smaller. I will love God with my whole heart and soul, and I will stand firm in His love for me. I will always listen to the still, small voice of God leading me out of the desert. I will run with endurance the race that is set before me. I will set aside every weight and sin that hinders me, and I will keep my eyes on Jesus, who is the Author and Finisher of my Faith. I will look forward to that glorious day when I am called home to be with Jesus and reunited with Jeffrey! I will trust God in all things, good and bad. I will never waiver in my Faith. I will bow my knee to God's Sovereignty. I will never let go of my Father's hand.

> *The LORD watches over you—*
> *the LORD is your shade at your*
> *right hand; the sun will not*
> *harm you by day, nor the moon*
> *by night. The LORD will keep*
> *you from all harm— he will*

31

watch over your life; the LORD
will watch over your coming
and going both now and
forevermore.
(Psalm 121:5-8 NIV)

Reflection

Spend a few moments and write out what you feel your own personal manifesto should be.

_____

_____

_____

_____

_____

_____

_____

7

THE LORD GIVES

I realize how God, who knows all things, delights in surprising us. In the middle of our darkness, He sheds His light and hope. During the darkest time our family has ever experienced, God gave us a gift. My second-born son announced that he and his wife were expecting a baby. The baby was coming in November. This news made me marvel at God's goodness, and the thought that the Lord *gives,* and the Lord *takes away* wasn't lost on me. Again, God knows what we need, and through our tears, our vision clears. Our family became excited about the coming baby. We soon found out the baby was a girl. The thought of a new

35

baby girl brought so many feelings to my heart. The first thought I had was about Jeffrey and how he would have been so happy about this news. He loved babies so much and was a wonderful uncle to his nieces and nephews. There were many times I had to swallow my grief and push it aside so I could enjoy this special gift the Lord was blessing us with. My life for the next few months was a mixture of joy and sorrow. Sorrow that Jeffrey wasn't there to share in our happiness and joy in the planning for this beautiful addition to our family.

As we approached the holidays, my heart ached. The sadness of those who have lost someone they love is intensified during the first holidays without them. I personally depended on the Lord to carry me through. It was the day before Thanksgiving that my daughter-in-law went into labor, and after many long hours on Thanksgiving Day, my sixth grandchild was born! The significance of this was not lost on my family or me. She is a gift to us straight from the hand of God to our hurting hearts. Her name is Lilian Rose. We call her Lily, which means purity, rebirth, new beginnings, and hope. She is a new beginning for our family. She has given us hope for the future and joy in the present, a living testament to God's goodness. I'm reminded of the verse Psalm 34:8: "Taste and see that the Lord is good; blessed are those who take refuge in Him."

I have taken refuge in Him this past year, and I can say I am blessed beyond measure, and I thank God for His goodness. Blessed be the name of the Lord.

◆———— Reflection ————◆

How have you taken refuge in Him during this difficult time?

_____

_____

_____

_____

_____

_____

_____

8

THE SMALL THINGS

Our Heavenly Father sees all, knows all, and controls all. He knows us from our mother's womb. He knows how many hairs are on our heads. He knows our every thought. He loves us with tenderness and fierceness that rivals any great love this world has to offer because His love is an everlasting love.

I am in awe of God's lovingkindness in my life. A few months before our son Jeffrey died, we had two cats named Cheeto and Bandit. Cheeto was an orange tabby who was sweet, gentle, and

41

loving. In fact, during the Covid lockdown, I passed the time by teaching him a few tricks like how to give high fives, jump through hoops, and silly things like that. Suddenly one day, he stopped eating, refusing even his favorite food. I took him to two different vets and the animal hospital, only to be told there was nothing they could do for him. He was experiencing kidney failure, and his organs were shutting down. The vet advised me to do the kindest thing, put him down. It was obvious Cheeto was suffering and had begun struggling to breathe and was whimpering, so I proceeded to take him home so my husband and son could say their goodbyes. It was such a hard thing for me to do, and I cried for weeks. Little did I know how sorrow would visit me again.

Fast forward two months, and I got the news about my son Jeffrey's passing. At the time, my husband and I were living in Alaska, and three of my sons were living in Texas. Family members flew to Texas to help with Jeffrey's memorial service and be together.

Jeffrey had a cat of his own. A Bengal cat named Dirk. The cat was with Jeffrey when he died, so it was experiencing some trauma as well. I guess all of us were grieving. I don't know if animals grieve, but after witnessing my son's cat, I do think they experience some sort of loss.

I decided to bring the cat back to Alaska with me. We knew how much Jeff had loved that cat. There were many videos and pictures of Jeffrey with Dirk either sitting on his lap or snuggling on a couch. My husband and I knew Jeffrey would never want Dirk to end up in the pound. So, I brought him home and introduced him to Bandit. It took a while for Dirk to get used to his new environment and feel better. I'm sure all the changes in his life left him scared and confused, much like his human family. I had some of Jeffrey's t-shirts that I often let Dirk sleep on where he could pick up Jeffrey's scent. He would

43

snuggle on those shirts and fall asleep. It was one of the sweetest things I have ever witnessed, and I knew Dirk missed Jeffrey.

This whole situation with Dirk is another example of the goodness of God. It made me see how God cares for all of us, including His creation. I realized if Cheeto hadn't passed away two months earlier, we would never have had room for Dirk. We just *couldn't* have three cats! That would push me into the "cat lady" status, which my family says I already am—with or without Dirk.

The biggest blessing we have experienced in having Dirk is that he's a daily reminder of Jeffrey. I love taking care of Dirk, knowing it's something Jeffrey would have wanted.

I can see God's kindness to us, even in a little thing like a cat. The Bible says, "And we know that all things work together[a] for good for those who love God, who are called according to his purpose" (Romans 8:28).

44

Dirk has been an instrument of healing to my husband and me. Loving something our son loved just feels right, and our whole family feels the same way.

What a beautiful example of the Lord giving us something to help mend our broken hearts and continue each day without Jeffrey. I don't know if people from Heaven can catch glimpses of earth, but if they do, then I know Jeffrey is laughing at the fun Dirk and Bandit are having together, and that makes my heart lighter, at least for today.

◆——— Reflection ———◆

What small things has God done for you that
have turned into big things in your grief journey?

_____

_____

_____

_____

_____

_____

9

MOTHER'S DAY

*The steadfast love of the Lord
never ceases; his mercies never
come to an end; they are new
every morning; great is your
faithfulness.
(Lamentations 3:22-23 ESV)*

I was dreading Mother's Day. To me, it was just another reminder of what I had lost, my strong, funny, kind, beautiful son, and I didn't want to face it. My other children, husband, and friends wished me well that day, but there was a deep hole in my heart filled with a pain that no mother should have to experience.

49

I had received Mother's Day cards from all my children, but there was one of my boys whom I wouldn't get a card from—Jeffrey—and that thought was causing me to go under.

I decided to spend some time in my memory box and look at photos of my children when they were younger. I came across many adorable pictures of not only Jeffrey but of all the children. Most of them were of wrestling piles, goofing around, and silly faces. It reminded me that their childhood was one of happy chaos! The unexpected always happened. I cherished every moment of their young lives, aware that those moments too quickly pass. I was conscious of this truth, and it caused me to seek out adventurous, fun things for them to do, from building a playhouse in the backyard to jumping off cliffs at a nearby lake. I wanted them to be free, to have fun, and to be creative. Even though we didn't have a lot of money, they always found ways to enjoy themselves, and their big sister was a master at finding fun things for them to

do! To this day, I don't know how I fed them all.
It seems to have had five boys meant *always
cooking*. I used to joke that if I couldn't find one
of them, all I had to do was look in the
refrigerator, and there they'd be! Just the
thought of an average day in their young lives
makes me smile and laugh.

I count being a mother of six children to be a
huge blessing, and I wouldn't trade that part of
my life for anything in the world. My firstborn,
our girl Jessica, was a big help and influence on
her brothers' lives. As was the case in many large
families, she was kind of like a second mother. I
still feel like I need to apologize to her for her
brothers breaking every single thing she owned.
Growing up with five brothers, it's easy to look
back and see how the Lord used this in her life to
mold her into the incredible woman she is today.
I truly am so proud of her. She adores her
brothers and values all their personalities and
showers them with love for Jesus in a way that
only a big sister can. God was smiling on me,

helping me, and giving me memories that twenty years later would be the most cherished part of me. My children definitely are my pearls of great price. It's amazing the perception time gives you. Twenty-plus years later, I ask myself, *Did I love them enough? Did I encourage them enough? Did I teach them enough about God's love*? It is my hope I did. Every parent does the best they can. I know this to be true. Every parent makes mistakes. This is also true, but everything we do for our children is motivated by pure love. I remember thinking, *I would give anything if I could just have a clean house for more than one day.* My heart is smiling over that one because I would clean the house and then wake up the next day to a disaster area! I'll never understand how this happened. It's like they were little dirt monsters forming a tornado that rushed through the house every night! But I would give anything to go back to that time. To love them more, to hug them more, to speak to them about their

Heavenly Father's love more. That is why I am so thankful for my memory box.

As I sat with tears in my eyes, looking at pictures of them, I came across an old card. I picked it up, turned it over, and gasped as I saw it was a Mother's Day card Jeffrey had made in the first grade. There he was, smiling from ear to ear, holding up a sign that said, "Happy Mother's Day, mom, I LOVE YOU!!"

I crumbled on the bed holding that card, sobbing over Jeffrey and at the same time crying out my praise to God for helping me find it. Thanking him for allowing me the joy and honor of being Jeffrey's mom. I cried until there were no tears left, and I knew that God had given me a Mother's Day card from all my children that day.

That card is so precious to me; it's hanging on my wall to this day.

This is exactly how our Heavenly Father shows His love and goodness to us. In unexpected ways,

He answers the cry of our hearts and gives us peace. I live in awe of God's love for me and how He manifests His love in the midst of my grief. So, I repeat: "The steadfast love of the Lord never ceases; his mercies never come to an end; they are new every morning; great is your faithfulness" (Lamentations 3:22-23).

◆———— Reflection ————◆

Write down a few moments or memories that are
your favorite parental moment regarding your
loved one. How has God used these to help you?

_____

_____

_____

_____

_____

_____

_____

10

PHOTOGRAPHS AND MEMORIES

I took a lot of pictures of my kids when they were young. They grew up when the digital age was just beginning to explode. Cell phones were still kind of new, unlike now, where every teenager and ten-year-old has one. My kids didn't have a cell phone until much later. Cell phones were expensive, and we were doing our best just to put food on the table. I didn't trust cell phones. I always wondered what unseen dangers there were out there in that little box, but I am very grateful now that I have so many pictures. Every picture is a memory that brings

59

up happy moments in my life. Photos mean happy memories.

At times since Jeffrey died, I have often felt the opposite. Many photos bring up a memory of Jeffrey, and that causes me pain. Not only pictures but videos are all recorded and within reach at a moment's notice.

Jeffrey loved to make home movies. YouTube is filled with his many cinematic achievements. There are so many times when his picture or some of his videos pop up on my feed, and it always leaves me stunned. Sometimes I'm happy to see this. Sometimes it made me sad and caused me to grieve for the rest of the day. I feel shocked because I will accidentally push the wrong thing, and I'll hear his voice speaking through my cell phone only to realize it's an old video he made that I had been watching and had forgotten to close. My system will go from happiness to sadness to shock many a day.

60

Mary, the mother of our Lord, knew grief. The Bible states that she pondered many things in her heart. I can't even imagine what she experienced seeing Jesus on the cross. The pain and grief that she felt—so unthinkable. She probably pondered many things as she raised Jesus, which most likely served as a balm to her on that horrible, wonderful day Jesus was crucified. She had memories and pictures in her mind that brought her peace, words Jesus spoke to her that would prove to be a comfort.

I have experienced this myself, although on a different level. The Lord loves me and doesn't want me to be weighed down by grief. He's helping me walk through this with His grace and mercy every single day, including, if not more, on days Jeffrey's picture shows up on my phone or a memory invades my life unexpectedly. I know I can give that to the Lord, who cares for me with an eternal love. I can rest in that love; I can trust that love. I can be assured that "weeping lasts for a night, but joy comes in the morning" Psalm 30:5.

One day all our weeping will end. We will be face-to-face with our Lord and Savior and be reunited with our loved ones. All we have to do is trust in Him. He promises to wipe away every tear. So, I must wait for that day when I see Jesus. I must wait for that day when I see my precious son Jeffrey. I'm excited for that day, but in the meantime, I will wait patiently and with joy, knowing that death is not the end, but it is a marvelous beginning.

O death, where is your victory?
O death, where is your sting?
(1 Corinthians 15:55 ESV)

But thanks be to God, who gives
us the victory through our Lord
Jesus Christ.
(1 Corinthians 15:57 ESV)

◆──── Reflection ────◆

What is your favorite memory of your loved one and what have you learned from it?

_____

_____

_____

_____

_____

_____

_____

_____

11

THAT'S A SPICY PEPPER!

It took a lot to entertain five boys, and they were always coming up with crazy ways to outdo each other. One such event will be etched in my memory and forever make me laugh. My oldest son Josh had bought a pepper from Texas named the "Carolina Reaper." He placed a tiny jar on the table, which contained a hot pepper. The words *World's Hottest Pepper* were written across the jar, and the pepper measured "1,400,000 to 2,200,000 units on the fire scale." The rules were simple: whoever ate it won. The boys were chomping at the bit for their turn, including my son-in-law. Each one proceeded to prove they were the man of the hour! There was milk and bread offered to bring relief if they were so tempted.

One by one, they took their turns. The oldest nibbled a tiny corner and immediately was on the ground, nose running, sweating, fingers burning. And so down the line, it went, each one taking their chance to win the title. It was hilarious to witness. Up to that point, no one was able to eat the pepper other than a tiny bite. And then it was Jeffrey's turn. Given Jeffrey's impulsive nature, he grabbed the pepper, threw it in his mouth, chewed a few times, and swallowed. It took less than five seconds for the blood to rush to his head, and he was doubled over in pain, screaming, sweating, and breathing fire. We all looked at him in shock. Jeffrey had shown his superiority over his brothers. Respect was earned, given, and once again, Jeffrey held his place in the family as the leader of all things impossible.

I've always loved Jeffrey's "just do it" attitude. He applied this principle to many things in his life, and it proved to be an asset. People looked to him as a leader with heart. Jeffrey and I played tennis together in the summers, and he would always tell me, "Just do it, mom," "Don't give up," and "You can do anything if you don't give up," as he chuckled to himself because of how corny he sounded. He was always offering encouragement when I felt tired and wanted to quit. These encouragements still ring in my mind when I'm facing something hard. Never in my wildest dreams did I think I would have to go through the hardest experience of my life. Losing my son was so unthinkable, but I still hear him in my heart urging me to keep going.

So, Jeffrey, I will continue every day in the midst of pain and keep finding meaning in not only my life but your life and your death. I know it's what you want for me.

I don't know how many years the Lord has for me, but I want to finish strong. Most of all, I want to continue the legacy that was Jeffrey's life. That's why I'm writing these thoughts down. Maybe it will help someone deal with their own grief and let them know they are not alone.

> *Not only this, but we also rejoice in sufferings, knowing that suffering produces endurance, 4 and endurance, character, and character, hope. 5 And hope does not disappoint, because the love of God has been poured out in our hearts through the Holy Spirit who was given to us.*
> *(Romans 5:3-5)*

We do not rejoice *because* of our sufferings but *in the middle* of our sufferings. No amount of suffering can stop God's love for us, and if we preserver and press into God, He will lead us out of our grief to a new day. So, Reader, I know you are hurting, and a part of you will always be hurting but press on into your Father's love.

Allow Him to comfort you and lift your burden. And soon you will realize this verse to be a reality:

> *I can do all things through*
> *Christ who strengthens me.*
> *(Philippians 4:13 NKJV)*

How can you continue the legacy of your loved one? It can be as simple as planting a tree or bush, writing a poem or song, or ministering to someone else who is suffering as you are.

◆———— Reflection ————▶

Write out some ideas and allow hope to enter
your heart as God uses this to heal you.

_____

_____

_____

_____

_____

_____

_____

_____

12

CHRISTMAS

In Alaska, the winters are harsh, dark, and cold. It so happened that this year there was a blizzard. We had over twenty-five inches of snow in Anchorage in a span of two days. The snowiest December since 1950. It was a difficult time for most people. Schools and businesses were closed, and everyone was snowed in, waiting for the snowplows to come do their job. I remember thinking how much Jeffrey would be excited about the snow. He would have been the first one to run out and make a giant snowman. He also would have taken the time to

73

admire the beauty of the snow as it transformed the landscape.

It had only been nine months since Jeff had passed, and since Christmas was approaching, I wanted to do something special for him. I decided to make a Christmas wreath to leave at his grave. So as soon as the way out was plowed, I got in my car and drove to the cemetery. When I arrived, I was amazed at what I saw. The whole cemetery was covered in a blanket of deep, beautiful snow. It dripped from the trees and hugged the gravesites. It was breathtaking. I wound my way to my son's grave, which I could have found blindfolded, got out my shovel, and started to shovel a path to his resting place.

It's here in this spot I feel close to him. I know he's not there, but it's where my last earthly attachment to him is. It's here I get clarity. It's here I can also hear my Heavenly Father's voice of comfort. I try to put words to my jumbled thoughts. Thoughts of love, thoughts of missing him, thoughts of things I wish I could say. But all I can do at that moment is sob and place the wreath upon his grave. I suddenly hear the church bells ring out, and I am filled with peace. God lost his Son too, and He knows how I feel. I look around me at hundreds of graves wrapped in their winter blankets. I am the only one there. Jeffrey's grave is the only one adorned with a Christmas wreath. The contrast between the white snow and the red and green of the wreath is stunning. I don't know why, but at that moment, I am filled with hope and joy. I find happiness in doing this small thing for Jeffrey, this act of love. I wanted to add beauty to a place of death. I wanted the world to know God gives us beauty for ashes. I tell Jeffrey I'll love him forever and return to my car, serenaded by bells and feeling a familiar peace that passes all earthly understanding, and I thank God for Jeffrey's life.

Reflection

I know holidays are hard for us. It helps to write out some ideas that could turn our holiday sadness into moments that make us smile. Write out some thoughts on how to do this in your own life. Let God use this as a way to get you through the hard days and to create a new memory to replace the painful ones.

_____

_____

_____

_____

_____

_____

13

MAN OF HONOR, INTEGRITY, AND HIGH CHARACTER

Being a mom comes with many fears, doubts, and anxieties. We ask ourselves, *Are they cold? Are they hungry? Are they happy? Are they healthy?* The questions are endless. As a young mother, I was often in doubt of my ability to care for my children the way I should. I wanted them to grow up knowing who they were as men. This led me to consider . . . *What is a man? What are the most important traits a man can have in this world? What would make them stand out among the rest and help them be the men God wanted them to be?* I began to study God's word for examples of godly men and the character traits they carried in their lives.

I have always believed in "speaking life" over my children. The Bible says in Proverbs 18:21, "Death and life are in the power of the tongue," which roughly translated means we have the power to lift up or tear down with the words we say. It was very important to me to be able to lift my children up. To speak to them traits that would mold them to become men of God. I came up with three specific characteristics that I thought would lead them their whole lives:

Honor. Integrity. High Character.

Honor simply means to do the right thing. A man of honor is someone other people can count on. When given a choice, he always chooses the high road. If he makes a mistake, he owns up to it and does everything to make it right. Being honorable is believing in truth. A man of honor

80

sees people, respects people, and gives more than he gets.

Integrity stands for honesty, kindness, and reliability. These men do what they say they will do. They do the right thing when no one else is looking. They follow the rules. Having integrity compels him to help others and to put other people above himself. A man of integrity has trained himself to be selfless. To have a personal set of morals that guide him into a godly standard of manhood.

High Character allows a man to persevere through hard times. When things get tough, he doesn't give up; he keeps on going, looking to the finish line of life. A man of high character learns how to become a good friend because he allows honor and integrity to mold his life. These men are loyal people. They are not afraid of the unknown but are able to rise above challenges to reach success.

These three traits meld together into what a godly man should strive for. These are the things I wanted to see in my boys as they grew into men. So, every day when I would drop them off at school, I would tell them, "Be a man of honor, integrity, and high character today," I would speak this every single day, never missing a chance to speak into their lives. I believed in these words, and I believed this was what God wanted for them.

When it was Jeffrey's turn to go to school, I dropped him off and forgot to say these words because we were running late. He got out of the car and ran back, and said, "Mom, say that honor thing to me!" Little did I know he had been waiting for his turn to go to school and have me speak these words over him.

This realization blessed me beyond measure as a mom and helped me to realize how important this pronouncement was to my children. God had used my young son Jeffrey to assure me I was doing the right thing.

At Jeffrey's memorial service, many people came. Jeffrey's friends from his childhood, current friends, past bosses and current bosses, and many others. I was amazed at hearing these kind people share their stories of Jeffrey. They told countless tales of Jeffrey giving his time to help them in their life, often at a moment's notice. Stories of Jeffrey putting other people's needs above his own. Stories of Jeffrey giving more than he gets. Stories of Jeffrey persevering through hard times and never giving up. Stories of Jeffrey's humorous anecdotes. They warmed my soul and provided healing for our family. It blessed me to see Jeffrey was indeed a man of honor, integrity, and high character. It is my joy to know all my wishes and hopes for him are now fulfilled as he is complete, lacking in nothing, and he is home with his Heavenly Father. *Until we meet again, my dear son. I'm proud of you.*

14

PROM KING

P rom can be a big deal for high schoolers, and for Jeffrey, it was his time to shine. Being the flamboyant personality he was, Jeffrey decided to go to prom in a bright orange tux, complete with a top hat and cane from the movie *Dumb and Dumber*. Most of the time, I just shook my head at Jeff and let him go with his crazy ideas, but this took the cake. I'm not even sure how he afforded to rent this outfit, but he had a small part-time job, so I figured he could do what he wanted with his money. I actually had no idea he was planning this, as he kept it to himself. I remember snapping his picture that day, laughing at how silly he looked. There he was, dressed all in orange directing me as I took pictures. He was so happy at that moment, full of visions of the fun to be had that night. He was, of course, voted in as Prom King, and his outfit cemented him in his school's prom history. I remember hearing tales of Jeffrey's goofy behavior that night and laughing as I imagined him. Jeffrey was always the life of the party. People couldn't help but notice him, always smiling, always joking around, and always coming up with wild ideas. That's how he lived his life. He wasn't a "big picture" kind of guy. He was more of an "in the moment" kind of guy. He was everyone's favorite person.

Jeffrey stole my heart from the moment he was born. He was quick to smile and laugh, and his silly antics kept our family laughing continuously. He was pure joy. I am forever grateful I have videos of Jeffrey when he was a toddler doing silly Jeffrey things. They are my most treasured possessions, and on days when my grief is hard to handle, I will watch these, and my heart smiles. He was the light in our family.

I think about how God made my son silly, loving, and full of life, and I am grateful. I am grateful for the time I had with him. I am grateful that I had more happy moments with him than sad moments. I am grateful for the time he lived with us as a young man, figuring out his life. It was during these years that I witnessed his amazing ability to overcome hardships. He never gave up and always was determined to finish stronger than when he started. I watched him grow into a man of honor, integrity, and high character. I often told him how proud I was of him. I told him often that I loved the person he was. I told him often I loved him. Now I can say Jeffrey did finish stronger than when he started. He has run his race, and he has won. I will see him again, and for now, these memories are the balm to my sorrow, and I thank God for the joy of being Jeffrey's mother.

When it came time to plan his memorial service, I chose the picture I took of him dressed in his orange prom suit. It just felt right because it was who he was. Underneath that picture are the words "Everyone's Favorite Person." I know we will all be reunited with him one day, and for that, I, too, press on "for the joy set before me," and I am grateful.

 Reflection

Write out a few traits of your loved one. Things about them that made them special. Things that make you laugh. It helps to think about these things during grief.

_____

_____

_____

_____

_____

_____

15

WHERE I'LL ALWAYS BE

It's been almost a year since we lost our beautiful Jeffrey. If someone asked me when he died, I would think, *He died yesterday,* because no matter how much time passes, that's how it feels to me. We would trade anything to have one more moment with him. I hate the fact that life has moved on. It feels unfair to me on so many levels. Time moves slowly for me, and every morning I wake up, my son is the first thought on my mind, but the world around me is still spinning. They say anger is a part of grief, and I have experienced this as well. I'm angry my son left us. I'm angry he won't get to experience having a family of his own, children of his own. I'm angry that part of our family tree is snipped short and not allowed to sprout. It all is maddening and unfair.

So, I woke up this morning and did an inventory of my emotions. Where am I emotionally, mentally, and spiritually? I want to be honest with myself, and I must be honest with God. He already knows how I feel anyway. He sees my up-and-down emotional state as I live my life without my son. He understands my feelings, and He is patient with me. He knows I am angry at times, and He is near my broken heart. I often feel my heart will never heal. I know I'll never be the same. Every time I look at a family picture, my mind thinks, *This is before Jeffrey died,* or *This is after Jeffrey died.* I don't want to torture myself, but I think that's the nature of grief.

So where am I? I'm not sure I have the answer to that. But I do know where I'll always be. I know this is confusing because the question Where am

I? begs to explain where I am in this moment, on this day. I just don't have an answer to that, but I do know where I'll always be. Where I'll be tomorrow and the day after that and the months and years after that. The answer is simple. I'll be in my Heavenly Father's arms. He will hold me through this. He will comfort me; He will dry my tears as often as they fall. I can never exhaust His patience and love. The Bible says in Psalm 147:3 ESV, "He heals the brokenhearted and binds up their wounds." I know He is healing my broken heart. Because I trust in His Word.

There's also something I'll always be. I will always be Jeffrey's mother. I will always be holding him in my heart. I will always be in my memories of him as a little boy so full of life. These memories are getting a little easier to recall and are beginning to fill me with joy instead of sorrow. God's word also says that He "replaces beauty for ashes." (Isaiah 61:3).

I also realize where Jeffrey will always be. He will always be with me. He will be with me when I hear his favorite song, see his favorite snack food in the store, or watch a movie I am sure he would love. There are a thousand moments and memories that bring Jeffrey to me again and again. I am so grateful for this.

But more importantly, Jeffrey will always be with his Heavenly Father. He will never experience pain, loss, or fear again. He will never struggle with sickness or financial troubles, or loneliness. He will never experience the pains of growing old. He will always and forever be loved, fulfilled, and joyous in Heaven, away from the woes of this earth.

There is a verse I recently came upon that fills me with such hope. It's found in Revelation.

> *He will wipe away every tear*
> *from their eyes, and death shall*
> *be no more, neither shall there*
> *be mourning, nor crying, nor*
> *pain anymore,*

96

for the former things have
passed away.
(Revelation 21:4 ESV)

I look forward to this day, as I am sure many of you do. Dear reader, please know your loss is not the end. God has a wonderful promise for you. A wonderful hope where there will be no more mourning, crying, or pain. He will make all things new! So let God use this verse to penetrate your darkness and sorrow and fill you with hope. Go to Him. He can handle it. He can handle your anger, grief, and pain. He longs to comfort you. He longs to hold you and heal your heart. He is right by your side, helping you as you walk through this valley.

Come to me, all who labor and
are heavy laden, and I will give
you rest. Take my yoke upon
you, and learn from me, for I
am gentle and lowly in heart,
and you will find rest for your
souls. For my yoke is easy, and
my burden is light.
(Matthew 11:28-30 ESV)

97

Take these words into your heart and soul, for this is where you will find comfort and rest. I am praying for you. I know how hard it is, for I am living it every day. Together we will experience the day when all our tears are wiped away, and we are with our loved ones forever! I pray you find comfort and peace in this truth and are able to rest in your Father's arms. Amen, and amen.

 Reflection ━━━━▶

List some of the things you are angry about.
Then give them to the Lord one by one.

_____

_____

_____

_____

_____

_____

_____

16

I CAN'T, HE CAN

So many days I spent wishing I could undo Jeffrey's death. Wishing I could scroll back in time to see him again. Wishing I could change things. Wishing has brought me much sorrow and anguish. Everyone processes grief differently. We have all heard this before. I have witnessed it in my own family. I have come to believe there is no wrong way to walk through grief. It's different for a mother than a father; it's different for a brother than a sister. I also have come to respect the members of my family more as they travel on their own grief journey. I have been there to listen, to cry, to pray with, and to comfort them. At times, it has helped me as I put aside my own feelings to listen to them, to be there for them.

So often, I realize I just can't. I just can't think the unthinkable thought that my son is not with me anymore. I can't find the strength I need to pick out his tombstone, plan his funeral, or bury his ashes. Each hurdle I must go over seems impossible and unbearable, but I am reminded of a verse that states, ". . .With man this is impossible, but with God all things are possible" (Matthew 19:26 ESV).

There are a lot of things I can't do, think, or understand, but I have learned when I can't, He can. I must choose to trust in Him, who is the "author and finisher of my faith" (Hebrews 12:2 NKJV).

Matthew 5:4 says, "Blessed are those who mourn, for they will be comforted." God promises to be there for us, to comfort us with His Word and His Presence. It's something I am experiencing daily as I mourn my son. God knows I grieve for my son, and He also knows I grieve for all the things that I feel I lost at the death of my beloved boy. I grieve for the children my son will never have. I grieve for all the Mother's Days, Christmases, and birthdays I'll never get to celebrate with him. I grieve for all the things that will never be, but I am learning to put my hope in Christ from whom my help comes.

He is making this load lighter and more bearable in many ways. He is removing the boulders of grief I am carrying on my back one by one and teaching me to "Come to me, all you who are weary and burdened, and I will give you rest. Take my yoke upon you and learn from me, for I am gentle and humble in heart, and you will find rest for your souls" (Matthew 11:28-30).

◆——— Reflection ———◆

This burden is too hard for you to carry alone.
List a few things that you feel you can't do right
now. Pray over them. Put them in God's hands.
Draw on His strength to help you with each one.

_____

_____

_____

_____

_____

_____

_____

17

IT DOESN'T CHANGE ANYTHING

Recently my family received some news that would help to explain Jeffrey's death at such a young age. It has been unthinkable to even imagine what could have happened or why this happened. We sought answers to these questions for a long time and were never given anything that would satisfy. Even if we had something we could point to as the main reason, it would only raise more questions that would contribute to our never-ending trauma and grief. It truly is a circle of grief that seems to have no end.

109

I had talked to doctors, to the pathologist that performed my son's autopsy, and to many others in search of answers. I decided to let the pathologist conduct a deep gene test to see if there was something in our family's genes that contributed to this. Tests were done, and reports were created as a result. It was discovered my son carried a gene that was a mutation in his body that could have contributed to his death. This led to more questions and confusion.

I recently read somewhere that the human brain is incapable of understanding negative thoughts. We struggle to comprehend meaning when negative thoughts invade our thinking. I feel this is so true for those of us who must process grief. The main thing we struggle with is trying to make sense of something that just doesn't make sense. Death is traumatic and paralyzing. We are left with the fact that knowing the cause of our loved one's passing doesn't change anything. They are still gone. We hope that knowing will give us closure, and I understand the ache to grab at something, anything that will give us some peace. It's how our human brains work; it's how we process our grief. For me, the knowledge I received regarding this mutated gene led to doubts, questions, and tears. Was there something I could have done to prevent this? Why did this go undetected for his whole life? Why didn't we know about this? All of these questions just added to my sorrow and put me on a downward spiral. I felt hopeless, and I felt I should have known about this. After all, I am Jeffrey's mother! It took the Grace of Almighty God to shake me out of my sadness, questioning, and doubt. This is what I learned.

Death is not something God had designed when He created us. His original plan was to walk and talk and fellowship with us forever, free of sickness, sorrow, or pain. Then through rebellion, sin entered the world. But that is not the end of the story because God had a plan to save this fallen world. A plan of redemption. A plan of salvation. A plan to ransom us from our sins and once again join us into everlasting fellowship with Him. A plan to mend the broken mirror and give us a clear reflection of his love.

This truth causes me to look at death from a different perspective. I began to view this from an eternal perspective. The Lord started to show me verses to teach me. The first verse He showed me was "Jesus said to her, 'I am the resurrection and the life. Whoever believes in me, though he die, yet shall he live, and everyone who lives and believes in me shall never die. Do you believe this?'" (John 11:25-26 ESV)

God was speaking directly to my heart. "Do you believe this?" Yes, I do believe this. I believe this for myself, for my family, and especially for Jeffrey. I could feel the hope rising in my soul. God was giving me the only answers that mattered.

Another verse He gently showed me was John 14:1-3 ESV:

Let not your hearts be troubled. Believe in God; believe also in me. 2 In my Father's house are many rooms. If it were not so, would I have told you that I go to prepare a place for you? 3 And if I go and prepare a place for you, I will come again and will take you to myself, that where I am you may be also.

Those verses are such a great comfort and reminder to not be troubled in my heart. I had many things troubling my heart, especially right after Jeffrey died. These words soothed my questions and helped me envision my son in Heaven, walking on streets of gold, happy in the place God himself prepared for him. I began replacing my sad thoughts with thoughts centered around the Truth that the Lord was so graciously showing me.

I want to share with you one more verse that, for me, completely changed my thinking.

But we do not want you to be
uninformed, brothers, about

113

those who are asleep, that you
may not grieve as others do who
have no hope. 14 For since we
believe that Jesus died and rose
again, even so, through Jesus,
God will bring with him those
who have fallen asleep. 15 For this
we declare to you by a word from
the Lord that we who are alive,
who are left until the coming of
the Lord, will not precede those
who have fallen asleep. 16 For the
Lord himself will descend from
heaven with a cry of command,
with the voice of an archangel,
and with the sound of the
trumpet of God. And the dead in
Christ will rise first. 17 Then we
who are alive, who are left, will
be caught up together with
them in the clouds to meet the
Lord in the air, and so we will
always be with the Lord.
(1 Thessalonians 4:13-17 ESV)

I *would* see Jeffrey again. I do not have to grieve
as the world grieves, with no hope. My hope is in
the Lord. God gave me this promise. Jeffrey had
accepted the Lord, which meant he was in

Heaven waiting for me. This turned my thinking completely around.

I began this journey feeling everything grief is. Shock, sleeplessness, questioning, sorrow, not being able to breathe, living in a fog, and much more. On a daily basis, I felt like I was assaulted by my own sorrow and pain. I found as I sought out God's help, the fog was lifting, and I was beginning to breathe again. God was filling me with hope, and most importantly, I wasn't alone. He was with me, and He still is with me.

I will miss my son every day of my earthly life. But as I give this burden to the Lord, I find grace to get through the hard days. He understands my broken heart more than anyone, even more than my family does, and He is near me as His word reassures me:

> *The Lord is near to the*
> *brokenhearted and saves the*
> *crushed in spirit.*
> *(Psalm 34:18 ESV)*

Getting earthly answers to some of my questions didn't change anything, but getting answers from the Lord changed everything. My prayer for you is that you press into your Faith. I pray you sit at His feet, and let Him comfort you. Let Him speak to your heart. You are not alone; He is near you. He will never leave you. He feels your pain with you, and He is wiping away your tears.

 Reflection

List a few verses the Lord is showing you as you
experience your sorrow at losing your loved one.

_____

_____

_____

_____

_____

_____

_____

18

I CAN ONLY IMAGINE

One of my favorite songs is "I Can Only Imagine" by Mercy Me. Whenever I hear this song, it brings me to Jeffrey. I can see my beloved son standing in the Son, whole and lacking nothing. My heart knows he is in a better place; my heart knows he is where every believer longs to be. My heart knows he is beyond happy!

I go to his grave and stand over it, searching for words that are hard to find. So, my mind wanders to Heaven. It brings me comfort as I envision Jeffrey reunited with other family members that have gone before. I imagine Jeffrey in his perfected body, heightened mind, and fun-loving personality, tearing up Heaven. I don't know what life is like in Heaven, but I enjoy imagining Jeffrey pulling pranks on King David, running races with Elijah, and sitting at Jesus' feet, learning everything he didn't have time to learn on Earth. This is enough in these moments. There are many times I can't wait to be with him.

Sometimes I worry that I am more excited to see Jeffrey rather than Jesus. I feel guilty for thinking this way, and then the Lord gently reminds me He understands. God understands my perspective as I weep for my son. He is patient with me. He knows my vision is blurred. He doesn't judge me for thoughts like this. He assures me this, too, is part of grief. I will always long to see my son. My life is not the same without him. Our family has changed. We will always view life as "before Jeffrey" and "after Jeffrey." The Lord understands our desire to be reunited with our children because He feels the same.

We are His children. Sin has separated us from His loving Presence, and He longs to be reunited with us. The most comforting thought I have is this: my Heavenly Father knows how I feel. He has experienced the destruction and separation death causes. He loves us so much that even before the world was made, He had a plan to save us. That's a lot to wrap your mind around, but once you ponder on this truth, you will find yourself amazed and even overwhelmed at the love God has for us. He wants to be with us. He created us to live with Him forever! We are His.

There is a Bible verse that states, "But God demonstrates His own love for us in this: While we were still sinners, Christ died for us" (Romans 5:8). This means we don't have to be perfect to accept God's salvation. He reaches down into our mess and pulls us out into His love. None of us deserve this. Every person is a sinner. The Bible is clear on this:

> *The fool says in his*
> *heart, "There is no God."*
> *They are corrupt, they do*
> *abominable deeds;*
> *there is none who does good.*
> *(Psalm 14:1 ESV)*

> *If we say we have no sin, we*
> *deceive ourselves, and the truth*
> *is not in us.*
> *(1 John 1:8 ESV)*

I am so happy Jeffrey realized this truth and accepted God's forgiveness and salvation. I am so glad he didn't put it off until he was older. He didn't have that kind of earthly time.

I am forever grateful Jesus broke the power of sin and death by taking our place on the cross. He died an agonizing death, was buried, and three days later was raised to life, breaking death's hold on everyone who claims Him as their Savior and Lord!

.

It is true; I do long to see Jeffrey again, and at times this overwhelms me with emotion. It is hard to not have him in my life every day. It is hard not to hear his voice. It is hard to not be with him. But I truly can only imagine on that day when I am called home, I will see my son. I imagine Jesus standing beside him, both with silly grins on their faces, and I find *joy in jumping* into their arms! For me, this one thought makes me say, "It's all worth it," and I can't wait!

19

Happy Birthday Jeffrey

You would have been thirty today, my sweet boy. I woke up early and thought of you. I thought of how fast a year had gone by. It seems impossible I have been without you for so long. Our whole family feels your absence every day. Today feels like the shadow of your death is very strong. But as strong as I feel your shadow, I feel God's grace and mercy helping me. Dad and I went to your grave today. We left you a bottle of hot sauce and a wooden cross instead of flowers. That made us smile. When we visit your grave again and see that hot sauce, our minds will go to silly memories of you drowning your food in the hottest stuff you could find, choking and coughing your food down.

You have left us with many joyful memories, Jeff, and it makes this load lighter to bear. Thank you for who you were. Thank you for making our lives joyful and blessed. We all miss you very much, and we all will love you forever. So, on this day, I say Happy birthday, my dear son. It was a blessing to be your mom.

20

WHAT IS GRIEF?

I don't know what I thought I'd be feeling almost a year after my son's death. I have no measuring stick to use. I have no rubric to follow. All I know is I miss him. All I know is I want him back. All I know is my heart aches to hold him.

The Bible has many verses to help with grief and many encouragements that ease the ache I feel. Not only was Jeffrey ripped from me, but he was ripped from his whole family, from his friends. Grief is an emotion; it's a response to trauma.

It's a never-ending nightmare. Grief is like a
roller coaster with ups and downs and scary falls
that tie my stomach up in knots. Just when I
think I might be able to have a little relief, I find
myself approaching an uphill climb that I know
will throw me over a cliff. But I have come to
realize I am not alone. I know God promises to
never leave me, to never forsake me, and to walk
with me through every hardship in this life.

God's word instructs us, "We do not want you to
be uninformed brethren, about those who have
died, so that you will not grieve as the rest of the
world who have no hope" (1 Thessalonians 4:13).
We as Christians have hope inside us that we will
see our loved ones again. We will once again be
reunited with our fathers, mothers, sisters,
brothers, and children. This is a great source of
comfort to our souls as we go on every day in
their absence.

We still feel our loss all around our lives, but if
we focus on the hope that is within us, we will be

able to find joy in the midst of our sorrow. I am so thankful for moments, for memories of my son that materialize in my life, and I can smile. I can smile at who he was to us as a family and who he was as a friend. I can smile at the thought of him. I can smile at the hope I have that I will see him again.

Grief will never go away; it will never dissolve into nothing. It will always be a part of our lives, a part of our story, but it doesn't define who we are. However you are grieving, whether it's being alone, being around friends and family, talking to counselors, or crying yourself to sleep every night, just remember you are not forsaken. He promises to never leave us OR forsake us. For God has said: "I will never leave you, and I will never forsake you" (Hebrews 13:5). Grief softens our hearts for others, grief causes us to bow our knees before our Lord and King, and grief helps us dig into our Faith, to lean into His loving Presence.

There is nothing I wouldn't give to have my son back with me, to hear his voice, to hear his laugh. On those days when I'm overwhelmed, I grab onto the hope I have in God's word that I will be reunited with him again. I choose to believe God. I choose to trust in His word. I choose to have hope. My desire for you is that you will also choose the hope God has laid before you. Grab onto His Hand as He is your Savior. He will soothe your broken heart, and He will never forsake you.

 Reflection

How has God comforted you during your times of acute sorrow? How has He shown His Presence and love to you?

_____

_____

_____

_____

_____

_____

_____

_____

21

DEAR READER

Dear Reader,

It has been my honor to share my journey with you. Although it has been, at times, painful in the telling, it has brought me much happiness. Grief is experienced differently by every person. As I wrote earlier, there is no wrong way to go on this journey. You can have peace knowing there are some days you will just do the best you can. I have many days where I must willfully push aside thoughts of my son so I can do my job or finish whatever task I am on.

Grief is like a club that we don't want to join because the dues are the death of a loved one. It's too high a price to pay. I want to wish it away for all of you, as well as for myself. If you've lost a child, you are experiencing every parent's worst nightmare, and it's unthinkable. It's obscene to consider the reality we are living in but live in it, we must. We are assaulted daily on every side with triggers that send us back into shock and reduce our hearts to rubble.

I have mixed feelings regarding people who tell me it will get better in time. All I can think is that "time" does not hold my son, Jeffrey, in my life. There is no "time" that he will be in for me on this earth. The saying "time heals all wounds" doesn't refer to grief. Time will never heal my sorrow at losing my son. In fact, the more time passes, the bigger the impact of my son's death. And so, I wrote this book. I wrote this book as a legacy for my son. I wrote this book as a way to help you on your grief journey. To tell you what I have experienced in hopes it will comfort you.

I promise to pray for you. I pray for your peace, for your heart to mend, and for you to lean into God and His Word for your comfort. The best place for you to be is in His arms. He will be near you. He will hold you when you are crying so hard you can't see. He will dry your tears, even if you cry every day, until He takes you home. I never thought a person could cry so much, but I have cried every day in this first year without my son. Some tears are cleansing as I weep in my Father's arms; some tears are even joyous as I remember a particularly silly moment with my son. But my Heavenly Father dries them all. He sees me, He knows me, He loves me, and He comforts me. Reader, He sees you, He knows you, He loves you, and He comforts you. Lean into Him.

May God Bless you with every blessing. May you begin to have more moments of joy than sorrow as you walk down this path. He is a lifter of your soul. So, Reader, I leave you with two of my favorite Psalms. God has used these Psalms in this first year without my beloved son. I pray they will bless you and encourage you to know you are not alone and where your help comes from.

22

PSALM 121

I lift up my eyes to the mountains—
   where does my help come from?
   2 My help comes from the Lord,
   the Maker of heaven and earth.

3 He will not let your foot slip—
  he who watches over you will not slumber;
4 indeed, he who watches over Israel
  will neither slumber nor sleep.

5 The Lord watches over you—
  the Lord is your shade at your right hand;
6 the sun will not harm you by day,
  nor the moon by night.

⁷ The LORD will keep you from all harm—
  he will watch over your life;
⁸ the LORD will watch over your coming and
  going both now and forevermore.

(Psalm 121 NLV)

23

PSALM 91

Those who live in the shelter of the Most High will find rest in the shadow of the Almighty.

2 This I declare about the Lord: He alone is my refuge, my place of safety; he is my God, and I trust him.

4 He will cover you with his feathers.
He will shelter you with his wings.
His faithful promises are your armor and protection.

14 The Lord says, "I will rescue those who love

me. I will protect those who trust in my name.

15 When they call on me, I will answer;

I will be with them in trouble.

I will rescue and honor them.

16 I will reward them with a long life

and give them my salvation."

(Psalm 91:1-2, 4, 14-16 NLT)

Notes
Focal Scriptures by Chapter

Chapter 2: It's Not Right
1. Psalm 23:1-4 ESV

Chapter 3: The Hardest Time of Day
1. John 5:24 NET
2. Romans 10:9 NET

Chapter 4: God Decides
1. Proverbs 9:10 ESV
2. Job 42:1-2 NET
3. Job 1:21 NET

Chapter 5: Joy in Jumping
1. Matthew 7:25 NET

Chapter 6: Manifesto
1. Psalm 121:5-8 NIV

Chapter 7: The Lord Gives
1. Psalm 34:8 NET

Chapter 8: The Small Things
1. Romans 8:28 NET

Chapter 9: Mother's Day
1. Lamentations 3:22-23 ESV

Chapter 10: Photographs and Memories

1. Psalm 30:5 NET
2. 1 Corinthians 15:55 ESV
3. 1 Corinthians 15:57 ESV

Chapter 11: That's a Spicy Pepper!
1. Romans 5:3-5 NET
2. Philippians 4:13 NKJV

Chapter 13: Man of Honor, Integrity, and High Character
1. Proverbs 18:21 NET

Chapter 15: Where I'll Always Be
1. Psalm 147:3 ESV
2. Isaiah 61:3 NET
3. Revelation 21:4 ESV
4. Matthew 11:28-30 ESV

Chapter 16: I Can't, He Can
1. Matthew 19:26 ESV
2. Hebrews 12:2 NKJV
3. Matthew 5:4 NET

Chapter 17: It Doesn't Change Anything
1. John 11:25-26 ESV
2. John 14:1-3 ESV
3. 1 Thessalonians 4:13-18 ESV
4. Psalm 34:18 ESV

Chapter 18: I Can Only Imagine
1. Psalm 14:1 ESV
2. 1 John 1:8 ESV

Chapter 20: What is Grief?
1. 1 Thessalonians 4:13 NET
2. Hebrews 13:5 NET

Chapter 22: Psalm 121 NLV

Chapter 23: Psalm 91 NLT

Pictures with Jeffrey

Family fun night -
March 23, 2018

Jeffrey with Dirk -
March 24, 2022

Brothers in arms -
April 14, 2022

Prom King